The HEART of ROSES QUILT

The Heart of Roses Quilt

C. Jean Horst

Good Books

Intercourse, PA 17534

Acknowledgments and Special Thanks to:

My mother who encouraged me from early childhood to believe that my creative energies
had value and that, "Anything worth doing is worth doing right."

My mother-in-law who connected my sewing background with her confidence that I could piece a quilt.

My husband who had enough insight and faith in me to see past the initial investment needed
to start a quilt business and who laboriously helped me computerize my accounts and inventory.

Our daughter and two sons for their patience and understanding in dealing with my home business.

The Old Country Store and their staff for promoting my work
in their quaint but beautiful store in Intercourse, the heart of Lancaster County, Pennsylvania.

The staff of Good Books and those who made this book a possibility:
Merle Good, Phyllis Good, Cheryl Benner, Dawn Ranck, Kenny Pellman, and Rachel Pellman.

Cover design by Dawn J. Ranck
Design by Cheryl Benner and Dawn J. Ranck
Cover and color photography by Jonathan Charles

HEART OF ROSES QUILT
© 1994 by Good Books, Intercourse, PA 17534
International Standard Book Number: 1-56148-106-8
Library of Congress Catalog Card Number: 94-36558

Library of Congress Cataloging-in-Publication Data
Horst, C. Jean.
    The heart of roses quilt / C. Jean Horst.
        p. cm.
    ISBN 1-56148-106-8
    1. Applique--Patterns. 2. Quilting--Patterns. 3. Roses in art.
I. Title.
TT779.H67   1994
746.46--dc20   94-36558
                                          CIP

Table of Contents

The Heart of Roses Quilt

How the Heart of Roses Pattern Came to Be

When, at the age of five, I made a disappointing attempt to create doll clothes, my mother patiently taught me to use her sewing machine. I have been sewing ever since.

Yet it was on a family vacation 33 years later that I first discovered the creative and colorful world of quilts. I live in Lancaster County, Pennsylvania, an area rich with a tradition of quiltmaking, but I had somehow missed it. Two fully stocked fabric stores lie only a few miles from my home, but it was in a little quilt shop in Gatlinburg, Tennessee, that I purchased my first quilt pattern, at the gentle urging of my mother-in-law, who was with me.

Home from vacation, I went straight to the fabric store. One week later I had pieced what I thought was the most beautiful quilt in the world—the Modernistic Star—in red, white, and blue. Knowing nothing about quilting, I called my neighbor who saw to the quilting. Before I knew what happened, I sold it. Somewhere in this world is the quilt that opened my eyes to how satisfying and creative this hobby could be. It proved to be the hiding place for the quilt bug that had severely bitten me.

Weeks later, with great enthusiasm and little thought, I placed a small ad in *The Penny Saver,* a local weekly newspaper, asking for experienced help to piece quilt tops. Amish and Mennonite women from local towns began calling. I had a true education as I met with them in their homes and learned about their favorite quilt patterns, as well as ways to process grape juice, make butter, use a treadle sewing machine, grow pansies from saved seeds, and dry apples for snitz. A whole new world opened to me—right in my own backyard.

Now, eight years later, my hobby has become a business. I work with many ambitious women who piece, applique, mark, quilt, and bind quilts and wall hangings, creating heirlooms for tomorrow and functional art for today. As I worked with traditional patterns, I began to imagine others. I wanted to create an applique pattern that was original, yet based upon a centuries' old flower—the rose. Not only did I enjoy the fragrance and loveliness of roses, I have always admired red and green quilts.

And so, after much experimenting, I completed my Heart of Roses pattern. The quilt was warmly and widely received, and soon I began receiving requests for the pattern itself.

One day, the staff of The Old Country Store (where I sell many of my quilts) was asked by a customer for a wall-sized version of the Heart of Roses quilt. I discovered that by adapting the original pattern and focusing upon the central motif, I had a design of exactly One Dozen Roses!

The delicate pattern was appliqued and quilted—and sold repeatedly. Once again, I began receiving requests for this pattern.

What a pleasure to offer both patterns—the Heart of Roses and One Dozen Roses—in the same book! They are here in full-sized patterns with clear instructions, for the pleasure of the beginner or the experienced quiltmaker.

THE HEART OF ROSES QUILT
Fabric Requirements

Background yardage
- 3⅓ yards—116"-wide fabric—total yardage for quilt top
- 3⅓ yards—116"-wide fabric—for seamless quilt backing

Helpful Tip

Wide 116" fabric allows a seamless top panel, as well as a seamless quilt back. You may not be able to obtain wide fabric in all locations, so you may order a Background Fabric Pack (available in four bed sizes) from The Old Country Store, P.O. Box 419, Intercourse, PA 17534, 1/800/760-7171. See order form on page 95 of this book.

King mattress, 78" x 80"	approx. quilted size—110" x 110"
California King mattress, 72" x 84"	approx. quilted size—104" x 114"
Queen mattress, 60" x 80"	approx. quilted size—92" x 109"
Double mattress, 54" x 75"	approx. quilted size—87" x 105"

Background Fabric Pack for the Heart of Roses Quilt from The Old Country Store includes:
- Ivory 50% poly/50% cotton blend fabric, preshrunk, permanent press
- 1 precut pillow throw with stenciled feather heart design
- 1 precut center panel with large stenciled scalloped heart, stenciled center feather heart design, center rose with ½" and 1" crosshatching, stenciled feather heart design in two lower corners
- 1 precut bottom border
- 2 precut side borders
- 1 seamless quilt back of matching wide fabric (wider and longer than quilt top size)

Applique Yardage—45"-wide fabric
¼ yd. dark solid—Rosebud center, heart frame
¼ yd. each of two prints of medium shades—Inner Rosebud
¼ yd. each of two light prints—Outer Rose petals
¼ yd. dark solid—Rose leaves
¼ yd. light solid—Bud leaves
¼ yd. contrasting print—Bell flower, Center heart, Pillow hearts
1¼ yds. of solid—Binding
2 skeins of embroidery floss—Berries
1 skein of embroidery floss—Berry stems
1 pkg. single fold bias tape—Stems (folded and ironed to ¼")

ONE DOZEN ROSES WALL QUILT
Fabric Requirements
(using 45"-wide fabric)

1¼ yds. background fabric—Background of wall quilt

¼ yd. solid—Rose centers, heart frame

¼ yd. each of two prints of medium shades—Inner Rosebud, heart

¼ yd. each of two light prints—Outer Rose petals

¼ yd. dark solid—Rose leaves

¼ yd. light solid—Bud leaves

2 yds. solid or print—Border and binding

1 pkg. single fold bias tape—Stems (folded and ironed to ¼")

2 skeins embroidery floss—Berries

1 skein embroidery floss—Stems

Prewashing Colored Fabrics

Check if fabrics are colorfast by wetting each piece separately and placing it on a white paper towel for several minutes. If bleeding occurs, wash and dry the pieces separately. For best results, check all bleeding fabrics again after they have been washed and replace any that are not colorfast.

Making Templates

1. The applique templates in this book are given in actual size, without seam allowances. Trace them that way. (Quilters use many materials to make templates, including poster board, sandpaper and cardboard. However, if you can find transparent template plastic in a craft or quilt shop, you will discover it to be durable, transparent, and easy to use.)

2. To use transparent template plastic, lay the plastic on the printed page and trace all pattern designs, using a permanent marking pen.

3. Cut out carefully and label all templates with appropriate names and letters.

HEART OF ROSES
Templates

A. Rose Center
B. Inner Rosebud
C. Outer Rose Petal
D. Bud Leaf
E. Rose Leaf
F. Bell Flower
G. Heart Frame
H. Center Heart
I. Pillow Heart

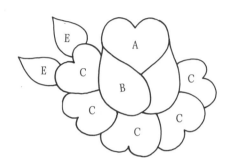
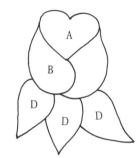

ONE DOZEN ROSES
Templates

J. Rosebud Center and Outer Rose Petals
K. Rose Leaf and Bud Leaf
L. Inner Rosebud
M. Heart Frame
N. Heart

Marking and Cutting Applique Fabrics

1. Using the plastic template designs, trace them on the right side of the fabric with light #2 pencil markings. Allow space between each design so a scant ¼ " seam can be added.

2. Cut each design separately, adding a scant ¼" outside the traced line for a seam allowance. This traced line will become the fold line, so trace lightly.

Helpful Tip
   If you cut the leaves from solid-colored fabrics, you can flip the fabric to applique, if the opposite direction is required. If you use prints for leaves, flip the template face down for the opposite direction. It is not critical on a free-flowing design that each rose-leaf grouping be identical. You may turn the outer rose petals and leaves in different ways so that each rose has a distinct look.

Cutting Layout for Quilt Background

All quilt sizes can be cut from 3⅓ yards of 116"-wide fabric using the following layout:

A. Center Panel—Cut on fold
B. Pillow Throw—Cut on fold
C. Bottom Border—Cut on fold
D.-E. Side Borders—Cut double

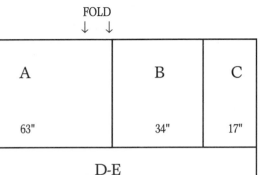

King Size

Mattress size: 78" x 80"
Quilt top size: 113" x 113"
Approx. quilted size: 110" x 110"

A. 63" x 40" folded (or 80" wide)
B. 34" x 40" folded (or 80" wide)
C. 17" x 40" folded (or 80" wide)
D.-E. 17" x 113"

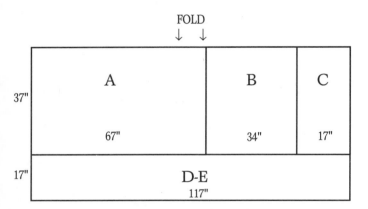

California King Size

Mattress size: 72" x 84"
Quilt top size: 107" x 117"
Approx. quilted size: 104" x 114"

A. 67" x 37" folded (or 74" wide)
B. 34" x 37" folded (or 74" wide)
C. 17" x 37" folded (or 74" wide)
D.-E. 17" x 117"

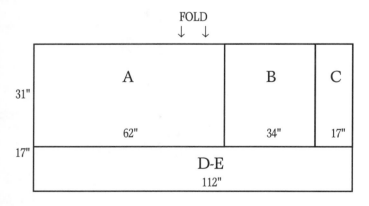

Queen Size

Mattress size: 60" x 80"
Quilt top size: 95" x 112"
Approx. quilted size: 92" x 109"

A. 62" x 31" folded (or 62" wide)
B. 34" x 31" folded (or 62" wide)
C. 17" x 31" folded (or 62" wide)
D.-E. 17" x 112"

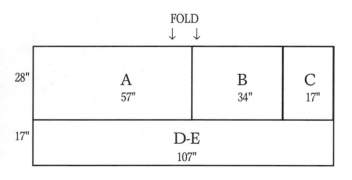

Double Size

Mattress size: 54" x 75"
Quilt top size: 89" x 107"
Approx. quilted size: 87" x 105"

A. 57" x 28" folded (or 56" wide)
B. 34" x 28" folded (or 56" wide)
C. 17" x 28" folded (or 56" wide)
D.-E. 17" x 107"

Cutting Layout for Wall Quilt

1. Cut background fabric into a 38" square.
2. Steam press crease line from fabric.
3. Cut 4 borders, 4" x 46" each. Cut fabric lengthwise to avoid needing to make seams.

Preparing the Background for Applique Placement

1. Cut applique/quilting layout designs from this book and match notches to form completed designs. Tape together.
2. Lay taped designs under background pieces, making sure to center all designs both ways. Trace lightly on right side of fabric for placement of applique.
3. Trace quilting designs now or after appliqueing is completed. It is your choice about when you trace them. Crosshatching lines are the most difficult to trace accurately if you wait to trace them until after you have finished the appliqueing. (In the Background Fabric Pack, the intricate tracing is completed.)

Hand-Appliqueing

1. Fold and iron the bias tape to ¼" width. Cut the size you need for each section and applique all stems in place, covering traced placement lines. The lengths you need will vary slightly.
2. Study the Layering Diagram on page 21 carefully, noticing the order in which you should layer the applique pieces.
3. Pin or baste the entire rose grouping over the placement lines traced on the background fabric, beginning with the leaves first and working toward the rose front. Notice that stitching is not needed when another shape covers part of the design. Layer in the order indicated on the illustration, beginning with all #1 pieces and ending with #4 pieces. For best results, finish one complete rose/leaf section at a time before you move on.
4. Turn under the seam allowances to the light pencil lines and applique with a ⅛" to ¼" blind stitch, using a single strand of thread to match the applique pieces.

5. For smooth looking curves and sharp points:

    a. Clip the inside curves and points to the seam allowance. This gives fabric the flexibility to spread apart and turn under smoothly. (Examples: heart center, rosebud centers, etc.)

    b. Stitch the outside points to a spot $\frac{3}{16}$" from the corner. To turn the corner, make an extra reinforcing stitch at the tip, slip the next side of fabric under the finished area with your needle, and continue stitching. (Examples: heart tip, leaf tips)

Embroidery Work

Finish the accents with colorfast embroidery floss. Use a stem stitch for the flower accents and stems, and a satin stitch for the berries.

The corner feathered hearts are a good place to sign and date your wall quilt. You may do so now with embroidery. If you choose not to add this identification, simply mark a small crosshatching design into the heart centers for a pleasing accent.

Helpful Tip

To create a fine, smooth, silk-like appearance, use only two strands of floss for the satin-stitch berries. Cover the area well with parallel stitches, going across the entire berry and keeping the stitches as close as possible so no background fabric shows between the stitches. When you leave one berry to start the next, do not jump across the open space on the back of the quilt because the thread "trail" will show through the fabric on the completed side. Instead, slip your needle into the wrong side of the finished stem stitches to get from one berry to the next.

Quilt Top Assembly

A. Center panel
B. Pillow throw
C. Bottom border
D. Right side border
E. Left side border

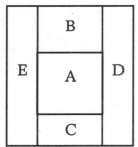

Moving in order from step A to step E, machine sew the pieces together with $\frac{1}{4}$" seams and thread to match the quilt top. (Pin each section well before sewing to prevent the fabric from shifting.)

Wall Quilt Assembly with Mitered Corners

Mitered corners are very attractive and not difficult to complete if you use the following method:

1. Cut the borders the length of the center panel and add two times the width of the border. (Example: 38" + 4" + 4" = 46")
2. Measure in from each end 4", the exact number of inches as the border width. Draw a diagonal line from that point to the outside corner and cut off the outer corner triangle. Repeat on all other

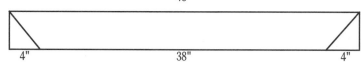

Cut off corners and discard.

corners, making sure the angles are opposite for each border piece (see diagram above). You will now have four identical borders with opposite angled ends cut to exact size.

3. Using ¼" seams and placing right sides together, machine sew all borders onto the center panel. Begin and end stitching ¼" from the corners.

4. To complete a corner miter, lay the border fabric with right sides together and match the angled edges. Stitch from the inside corner to the outside corner, using a ⅜" seam, taking special care not to stretch the bias angle. Press.

Helpful Tip

Match your sewing machine thread with the border color, not the center panel. This will prevent light stitches from showing on your mitered corners if your borders are made from dark fabric. Light thread used with dark borders shows only after it is stretched into the quilt frame—a bit too late!

Marking Quilting Lines

1. After you have finished appliqueing the quilt top, press it and mark it for quilting. (If you are using the Background Fabric Pack, most of the difficult marking has been completed, but you will need to fill in the long background lines and the border designs.) If you have not traced any quilting templates as yet, now is the time to do so.

2. Lay the templates under the quilt top and trace all feather heart designs, scalloped hearts, and crosshatching. Then do the designs for the borders and fill in the background lines.

3. An omnigrid ruler or yardstick, 1¾" wide, works well for marking all straight background lines. See the picture on page 7 for suggestions of line angles.

Helpful Tip

When you mark the quilting designs, remember to make the pencil markings as light as possible. Use a sharp #2 pencil point for clean, thin lines. If possible, do your markings on a light colored table top. If your work table is dark, be aware that the pencil lines could be getting darker than you think. To get the effect of quilt batting, occasionally slip a white piece of paper underneath the quilt top to check your pencil pressure. Heavy pencil lines are an ugly distraction on a completed quilt.

Hand-Quilting

1. Quilt stitches should be small and even, preferably eight to ten stitches per inch. Most quilters use a very thin, short needle called a "between." Betweens are available in sizes 7 to 12. The higher the number, the smaller the stitch you can make. A number 9 is a good selection for relatively small stitches and a moderately skilled quilter.

2. To begin, thread your needle with a 24" to 36" length of quilting thread and make a small knot at one end. Insert the needle into the quilt top approximately ½" from your starting point. Do not take the needle through all three layers, but stop it in the batting and bring it up through the quilt at your starting point. To pop the knot inside the quilt, give a gentle tug.

3. Outline-quilt ⅛" around all appliqued pieces, including both sides of the bias stems and one side of the embroidered stems. Quilt, as well, on all quilt markings. You can stack up to 5 stitches on your needle when you are quilting straight lines, but you will need to stack fewer for curves and feathers.

4. When you have about 4" of thread remaining, make a knot by the following method. With the needle above, but close to the fabric, wrap the needle twice with thread, insert the needle a stitch-length away from the last one, pull the needle into the top layer, and then pull it back out ½" away. This forms a knot against the quilt. With a slight tug, you can pop the knot inside the quilt. Trim the end carefully.

Helpful Tip
Use the needle point to hold the fabric taut while you pull, if the knot does not pop inside the quilt easily.

Binding

Scalloped Quilt Border

1. Cut 2½" bias strips to bind the scalloped edges. Bias binding allows fabric to conform to the curve of the scallop. To cut bias strips, fold one corner of the binding fabric down to meet the long edge. Press in this crease and, using the angle you have created, begin cutting 2½" strips from this fold.

2. Join the strips together end-to-end to make the length you need to sew a continuous strip of binding onto the three scalloped sides of the quilt. Make another strip to equal the top straight edge.

3. Trim the quilt edges before machine sewing the binding, using the scalloped guideline.

4. Fold the bias binding lengthwise to create a double thickness for durability. All seams in binding should be inside the fold.

5. Machine stitch a continuous strip of binding to the right side of the scalloped quilt edge, matching the raw edges and creating a ⅜" seam. Ease the strip along the outside curves and pivot at a point on the inside curves. The top edge of the pillow throw should be sewn last and treated as a separate side, using squared corners described under Straight Edge Wall Quilt Border, page 19.

6. Turn the binding over the raw edges to the backing until the binding fold meets the machine stitching on the backing. Blind stitch, just covering the machine stitching. When stitching the sharp inside curve, use an extra stitch at the point for added strength.

Straight Edge Wall Quilt Border

1. Cut 2½" wide strips of binding fabric, 45" long on the crosswise grain.
2. Join enough binding pieces end-to-end to create four strips, each as long as one side of the wall quilt.
3. Trim edges even on the wall quilt.
4. Fold the binding lengthwise to create a double thickness for durability. All binding seams should be inside the fold.
5. Machine stitch the binding to the right side of the wall border matching raw edges, using a ⅜" seam. Sew each side separately. First sew on the two side bindings. Cut the ends even with the wall quilt. Fold the side bindings over the raw edges so the fold meets the machine-stitched line on the backing. Pin. Then sew on the upper and lower bindings, allowing the bindings to extend ½" at both ends.
6. Turn the upper and lower bindings over the raw edges so that the fold meets the machine-stitched line on the backing. To square the corners, fold in the extended portion of the binding at the corners and blind stitch all edges by hand, covering the machine stitching.

Helpful Tip

Blind stitch with a single strand of quilting thread that matches the binding color. Blind stitching allows you to pull the thread taut and to create a strong hem. If you use regular sewing thread, be sure to use a double strand.

Signing and Dating Your Quilt

Take time to date and initial your quilt for future generations. Embroider or quilt the information into the quilting design in an area of your choice. Many quilters select a lower corner of the quilt backing, but follow your own preference.

The Care of Your Quilt

Your quilt is a valuable piece of art. The hours of work you invested in making your quilt should be respected. Appreciate its beauty and give it loving care to assure its long life.

You may clean it by vacuuming, dry cleaning, or wet washing it. If you wash the quilt, use a short, gentle cycle and mild soap or wool wash. To keep the colors bright, add half a cup of white vinegar to the wash cycle. Avoid excessive tumbling or wringing of the quilt. Air dry it, or use a dryer with a delicate and low temperature setting. If you machine dry it, rearrange the quilt several times during the drying cycle for uniform drying.

Old quilts must be given professional care.

When you are not using the quilt, store it on a hanger in a closet, in a cloth wrapping such as a pillow case, or in a cedar chest. Never lay a quilt directly on a wooden shelf.

A quilt must always breathe, so never store it in plastic. Roll the quilt so as to prevent permanent crease lines. If you do fold the quilt to store it, refold it occasionally.

Displaying Your Quilt

If you want to enjoy your quilt by displaying it on a wall, be sure not to expose it to intense sunlight. Direct sun rays can fade colors and weaken fibers.

1. Using the Dowel Rod and Sleeve Method

Hand stitch a narrow sleeve across the top edge of the wall quilt backing. Insert a dowel rod for hanging. Make sure your wall quilt hangs straight and flat against the wall. If it does not, make a second sleeve across the bottom back edge and slip a second dowel rod into the lower sleeve to give extra weight and stability to the quilt.

2. Framing Small Wall Quilts

Wall quilts look beautiful when stretched taut and framed. Cut binding 5" wide, fold it and sew it onto the front side as described in the Straight Edge Wall Quilt Border section on page 19. In place of the hand stitching step (#6), wrap the binding around a piece of foam core that is precut ½" greater than the exact size of the relaxed wall quilt. Foam core is lightweight, inexpensive, and readily available at any frame shop. Using a hot melt glue gun and clothespins as temporary clamps, gently stretch the binding around the foam core to the back side. Clamp the binding evenly around all sides. Then lift each clamp, one by one, and drop hot glue onto the foam core every half inch around the backing, clamping the binding again until the hot glue cools. Add a decorative frame to finish your piece of art.

3. Displaying on a Wall Quilt Rack

A 30-inch wide wall quilt rack works well for displaying larger wall quilts or bed-size quilts. Position the rack about 15-20 inches down from the ceiling. You can fold a quilt lengthwise and drape it over the rack to display a full wall-length section of the quilt. Many racks are available with decorative shelves to accommodate coordinating accents.

4. Displaying on a Bed

The quilt sizes given in this book have been carefully checked for accuracy and are designed with an approximate 15" to 16" drop along the sides and bottom of a bed. This will generously cover the mattress and will look best with a dust ruffle. If you intend to add a ruffle of coordinating fabric, nine yards of 45"-wide fabric will make a beautiful, full ruffle.

"Layering" Illustration for Rose

Arrange entire rose/leaf grouping. Pin well or baste.

Numbers indicate order for appliqueing. Notice that all edges that are behind another piece need not be stitched.

Only four templates make up this beautiful rose. Each rose can look unique by tucking the leaves and petals behind the bud center at various angles and depths.

Heart of Roses Quilt Applique Templates

Add a scant ¼″ seam allowance to all applique pieces when cutting them out.

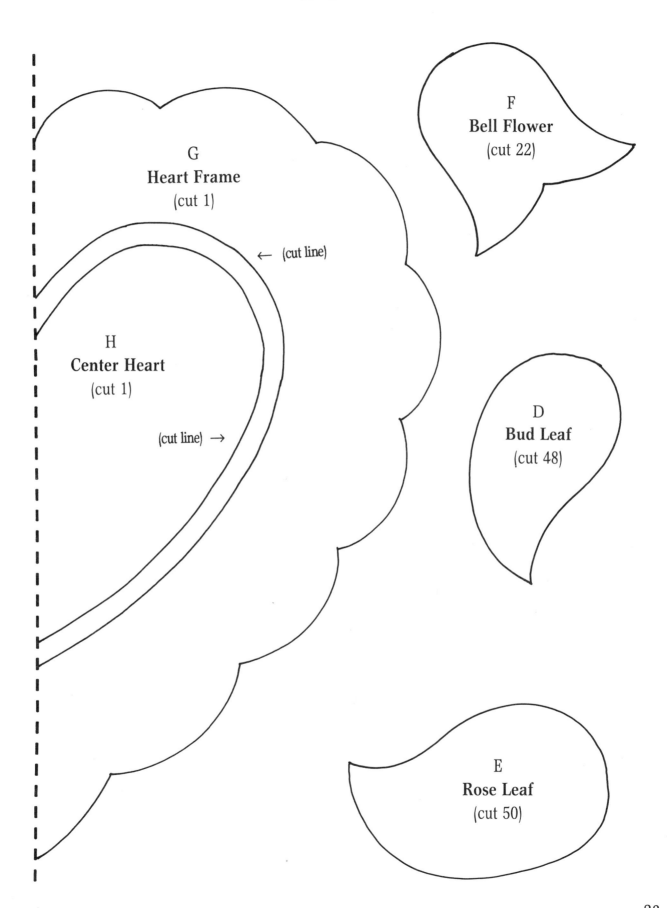

G
Heart Frame
(cut 1)

← (cut line)

H
Center Heart
(cut 1)

(cut line) →

F
Bell Flower
(cut 22)

D
Bud Leaf
(cut 48)

E
Rose Leaf
(cut 50)

Heart of Roses Quilt Applique Templates
Add a scant ¼" seam allowance to all applique pieces when cutting them out.

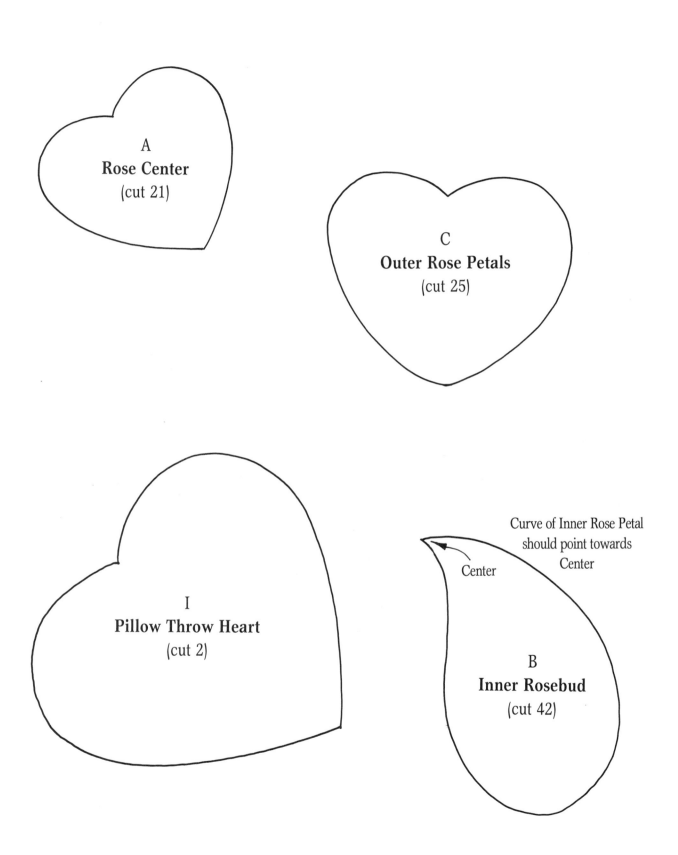

A
Rose Center
(cut 21)

C
Outer Rose Petals
(cut 25)

I
Pillow Throw Heart
(cut 2)

Curve of Inner Rose Petal
should point towards
Center

Center

B
Inner Rosebud
(cut 42)

X

Y

Z

Center line. → Flip design to create opposite side of design.

Cut along dotted line.

27

Cut along dotted line.

Center line. → Flip design to create opposite side of design.

S

T

X

29

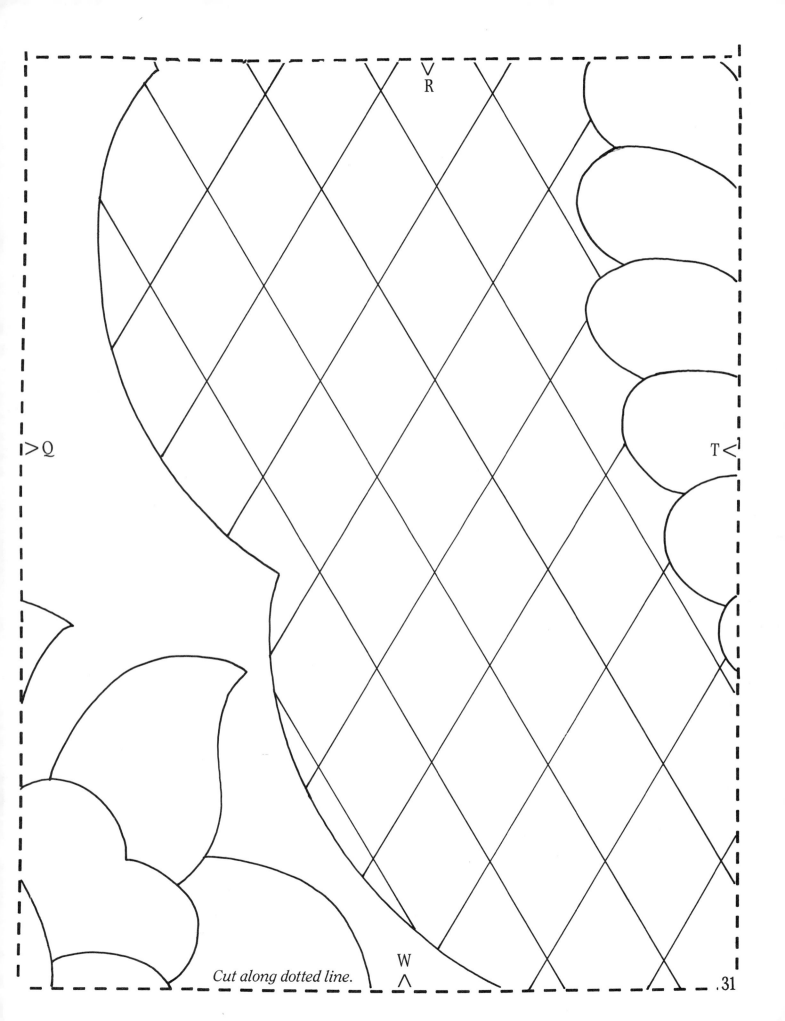

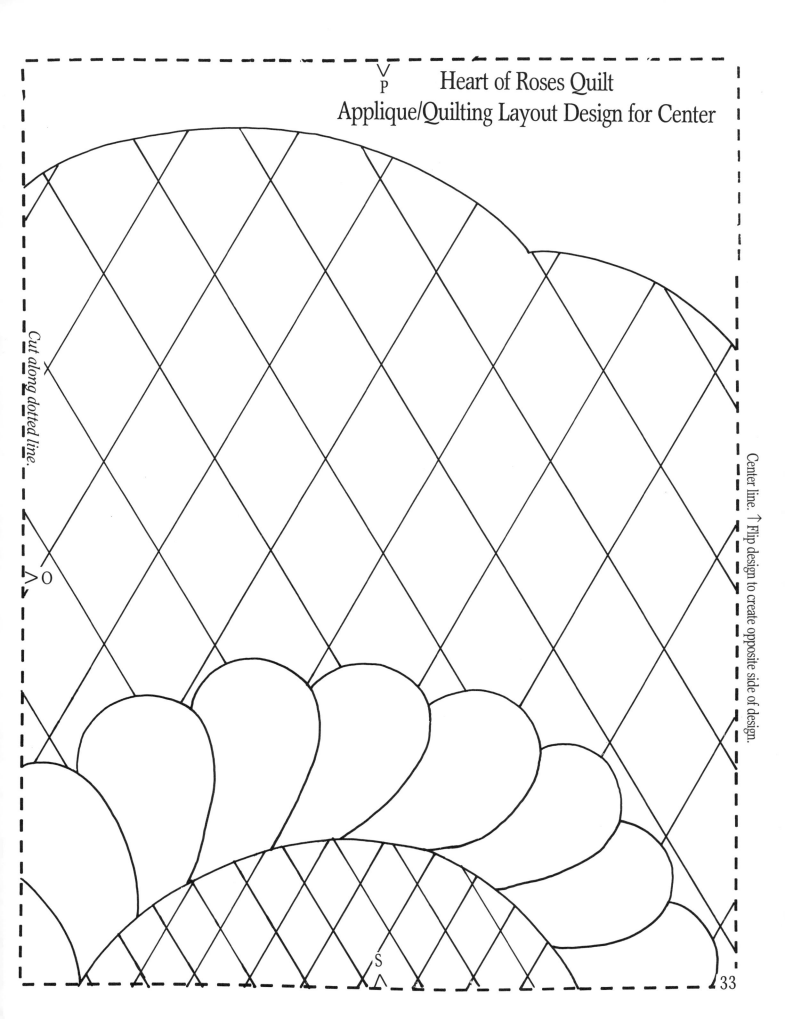

Heart of Roses Quilt
Applique/Quilting Layout Design for Center

Cut along dotted line.

Center line. ↑ Flip design to create opposite side of design.

33

N

Cut along dotted line.

Quilted Crosshatch Center

O

M

R

Heart of Roses Quilt
Applique/Quilting Layout Design for Center

> K

Flip design to complete opposite side of heart.

P

Cut along dotted line.

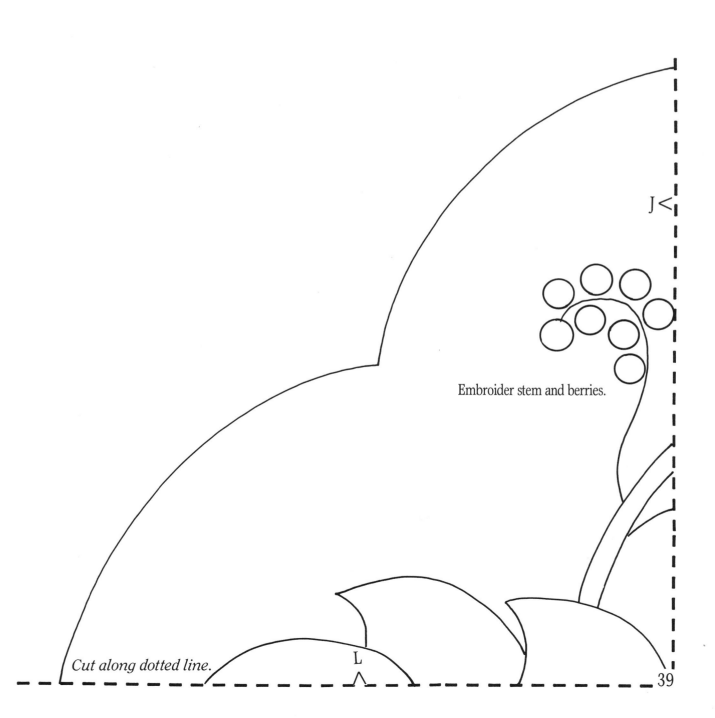

J<

Embroider stem and berries.

Cut along dotted line.

L

39

>J

K<

Embroider stem and flower accents.

N

Cut along dotted line.

41

V
L

Cut along dotted line.

M
DD

M <

D
∧

43

Embroider all berries with satin stitch.

CC

Create rose stems with ¼" bias tape or ½" bias tape folded.

D

Q

U

Cut along dotted line.

45

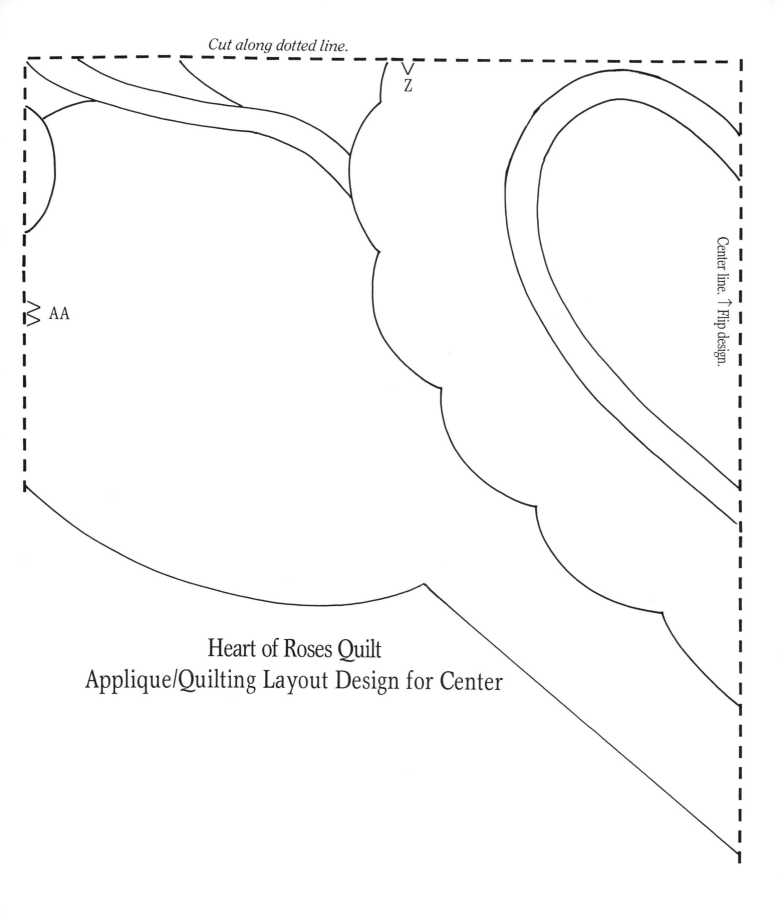

Cut along dotted line.

Z

AA

Center line. → Flip design.

Heart of Roses Quilt
Applique/Quilting Layout Design for Center

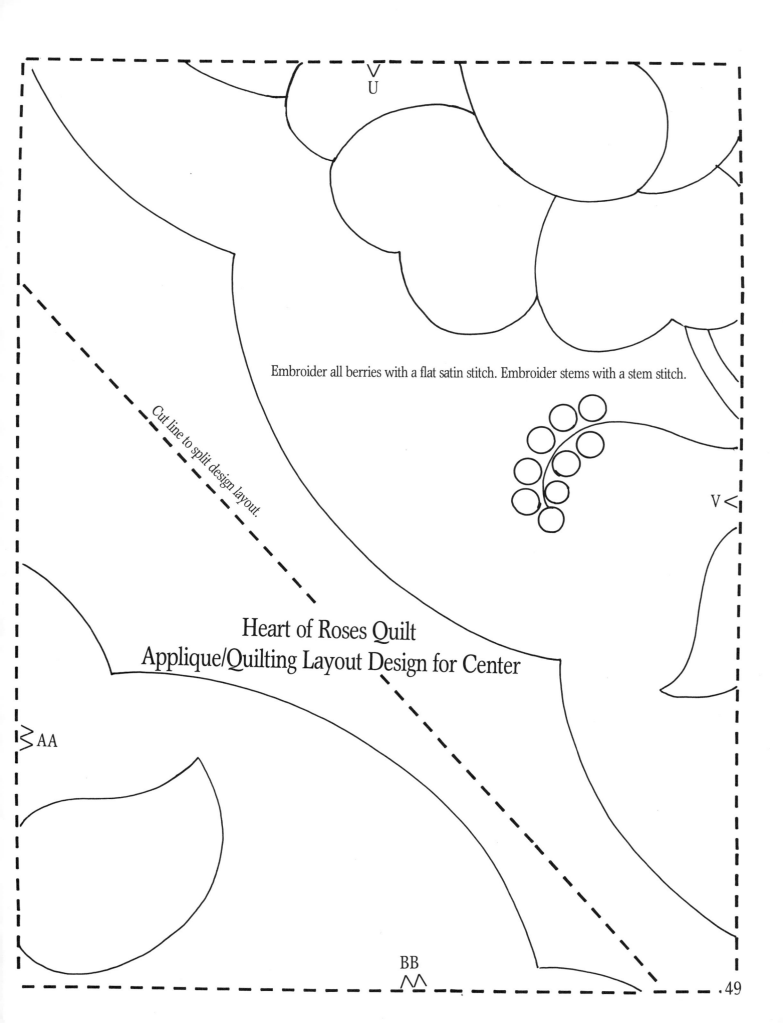

Embroider all berries with a flat satin stitch. Embroider stems with a stem stitch.

Cut line to split design layout.

U

V

AA

Heart of Roses Quilt
Applique/Quilting Layout Design for Center

BB

W

Heart of Roses Quilt
Applique/Quilting Layout Design for Center

V

Y

Embroider the centers of all the bell flowers.

Cut along dotted line.

BB

51

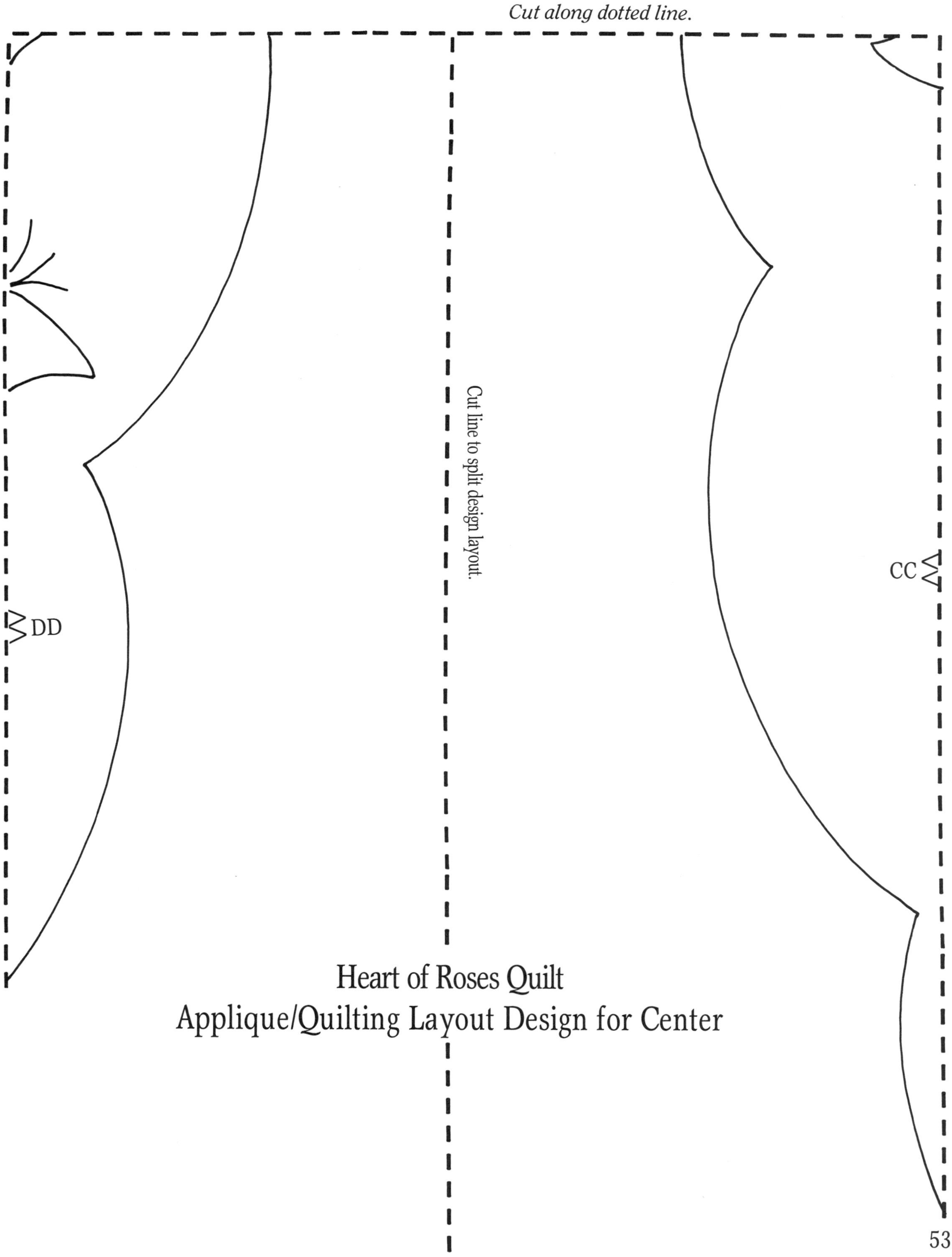

Cut line to split design layout.

DD

CC

Heart of Roses Quilt
Applique/Quilting Layout Design for Center

Heart of Roses Quilt
Applique Layout for Foot Corners

EE

Cut along dotted line.

Trace quilted feather heart design (from pillow throw) onto foot corners of quilt top.
Position 3" away from the side and lower edge. Arrange rosebud design inside quilted feather heart.

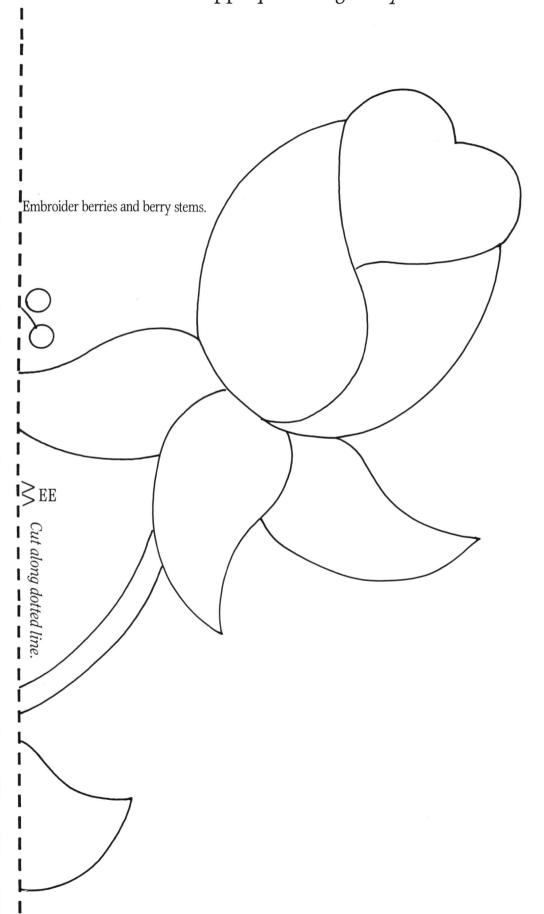

Embroider berries and berry stems.

EE

Cut along dotted line.

Heart of Roses Quilt
Applique Design Layout for Pillow Throw

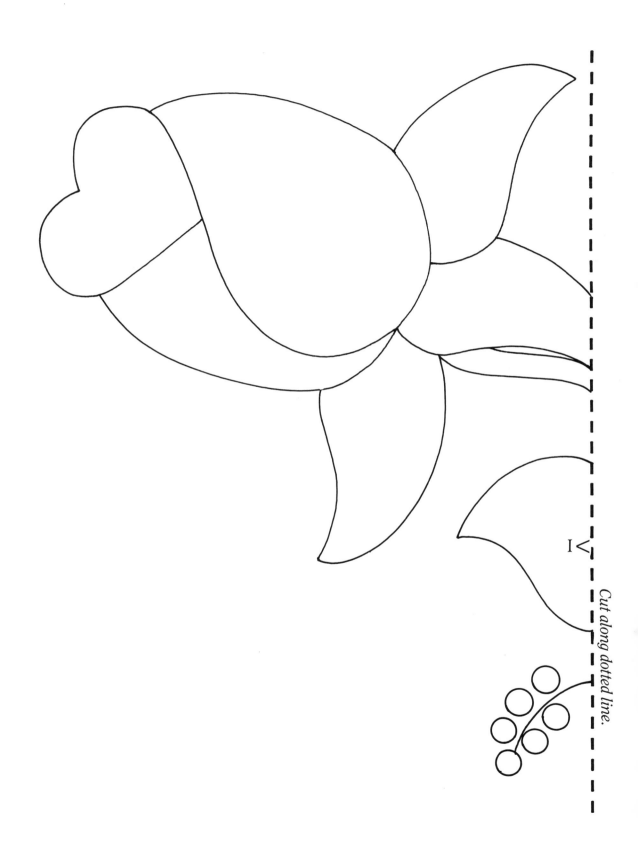

Cut along dotted line.

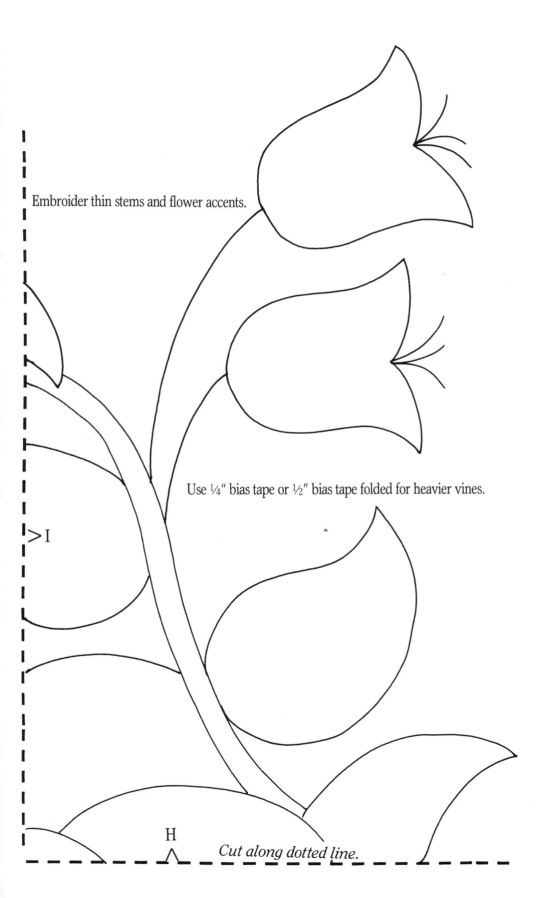

Embroider thin stems and flower accents.

Use ¼" bias tape or ½" bias tape folded for heavier vines.

>I

H

Cut along dotted line.

▷ B

G

Cut along dotted line.

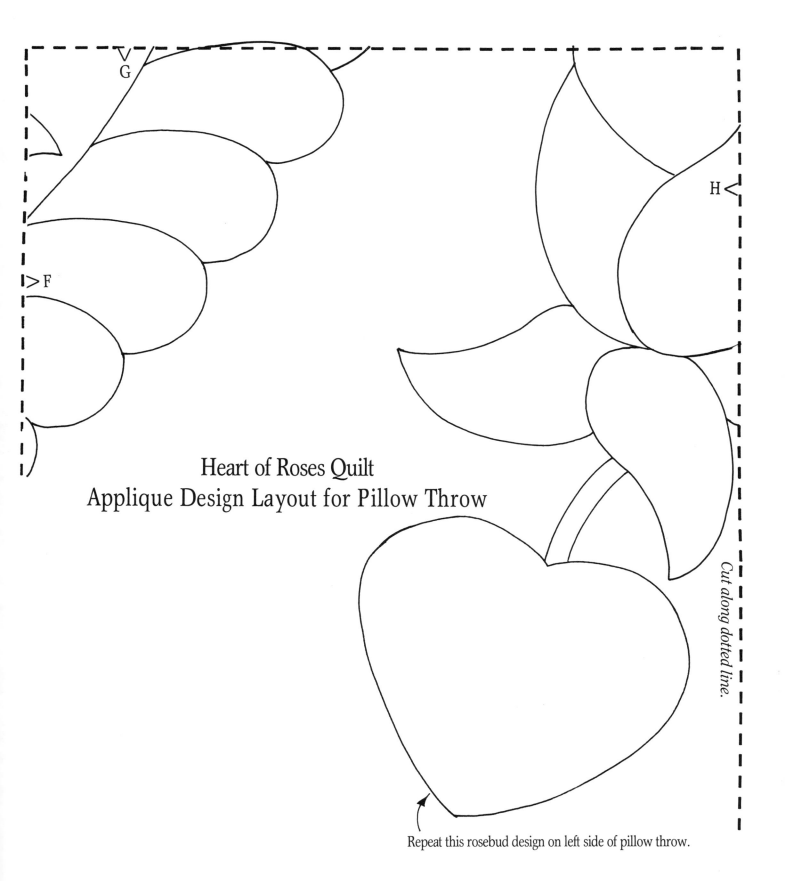

Heart of Roses Quilt
Applique Design Layout for Pillow Throw

V
G

H

>F

Cut along dotted line.

Repeat this rosebud design on left side of pillow throw.

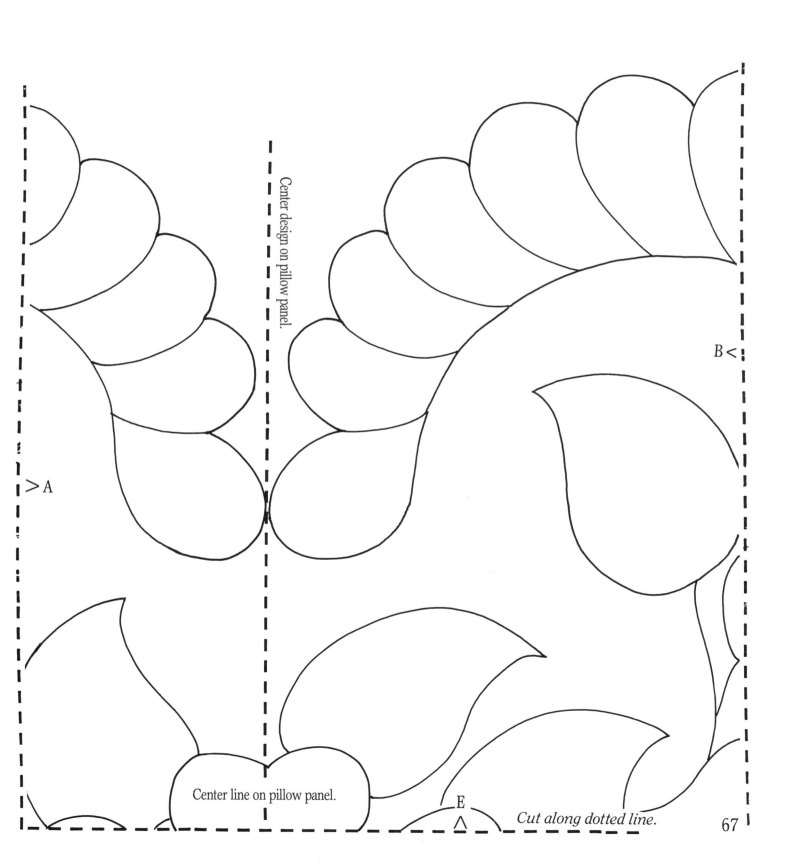

Center design on pillow panel.

>A

B<

Center line on pillow panel.

E

Cut along dotted line.

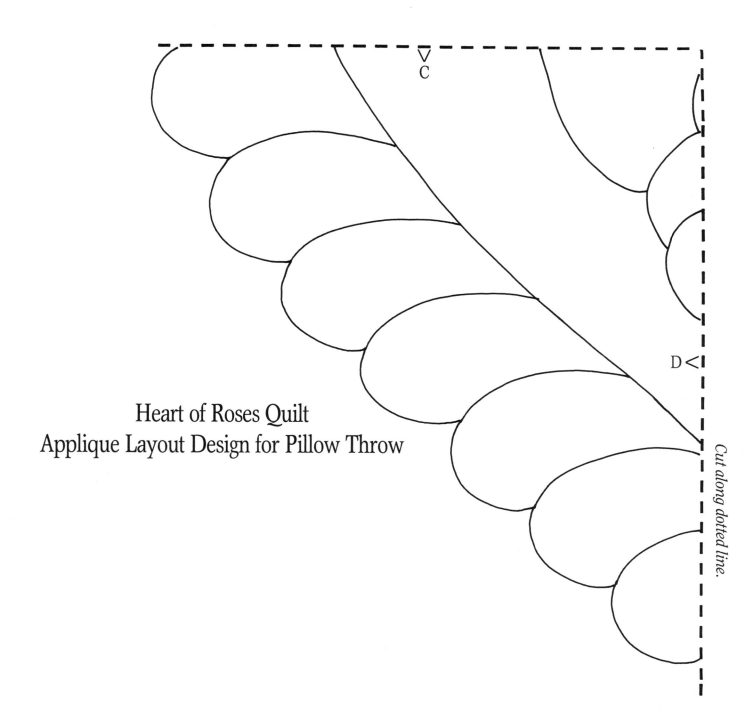

Heart of Roses Quilt
Applique Layout Design for Pillow Throw

C

D

Cut along dotted line.

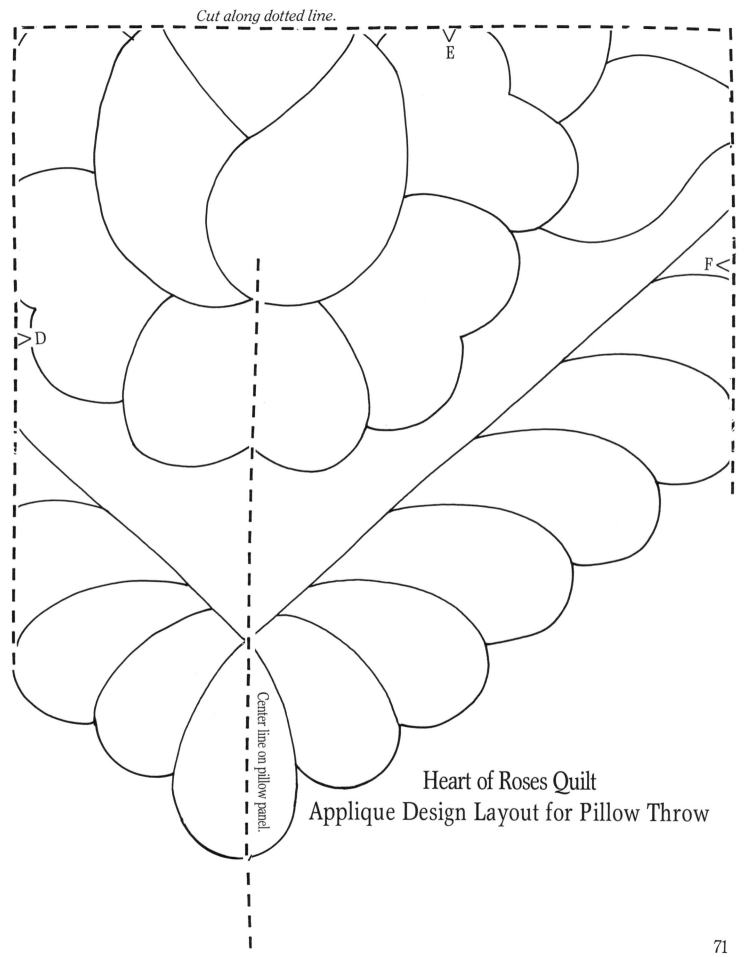

Cut along dotted line.

E

F <

> D

Center line on pillow panel.

Heart of Roses Quilt
Applique Design Layout for Pillow Throw

71

Heart of Roses Quilt
Applique Design Layout for Pillow Throw

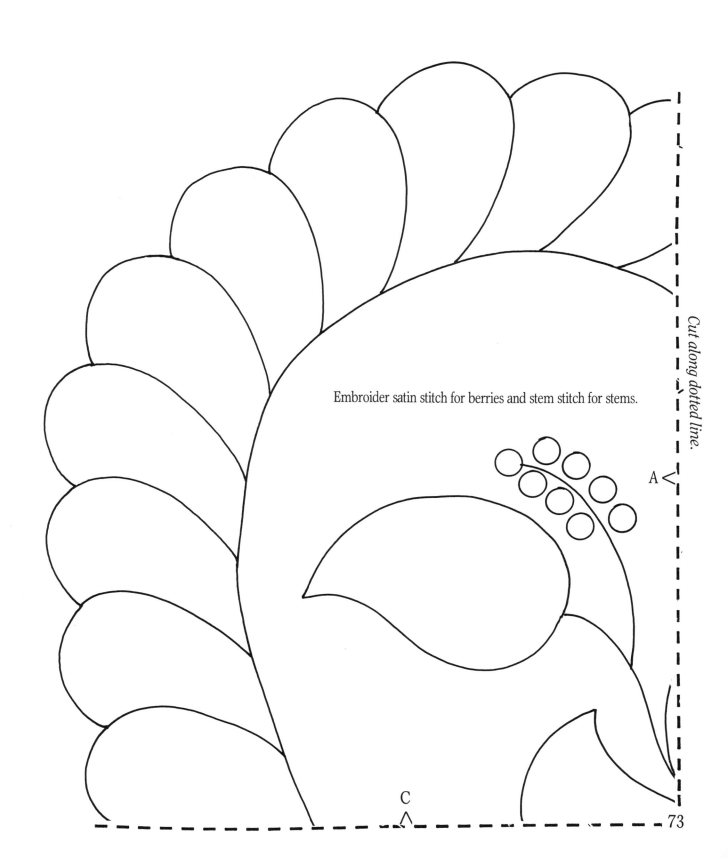

Embroider satin stitch for berries and stem stitch for stems.

Cut along dotted line.

A

C

One Dozen Roses Wall Quilt
Applique Templates
Add a scant ¼" seam allowance to all applique pieces when cutting them out.

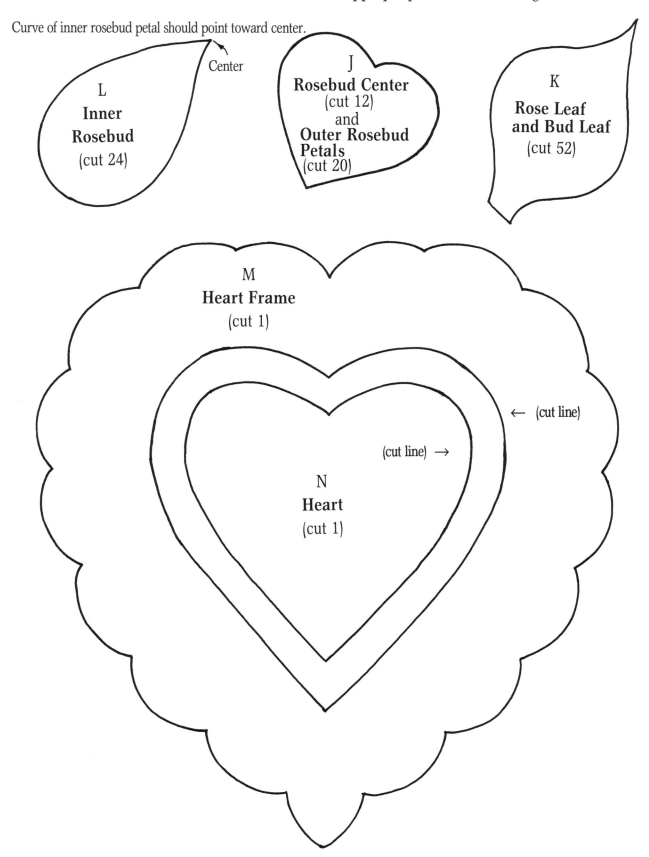

Curve of inner rosebud petal should point toward center.

Center

L
Inner Rosebud
(cut 24)

J
Rosebud Center
(cut 12)
and
Outer Rosebud Petals
(cut 20)

K
Rose Leaf and Bud Leaf
(cut 52)

M
Heart Frame
(cut 1)

← (cut line)

(cut line) →

N
Heart
(cut 1)

One Dozen Roses Wall Quilt
Applique/Quilting Layout

Cut line to split design layout.

Cut along dotted line.

MM

MM

FF

GG

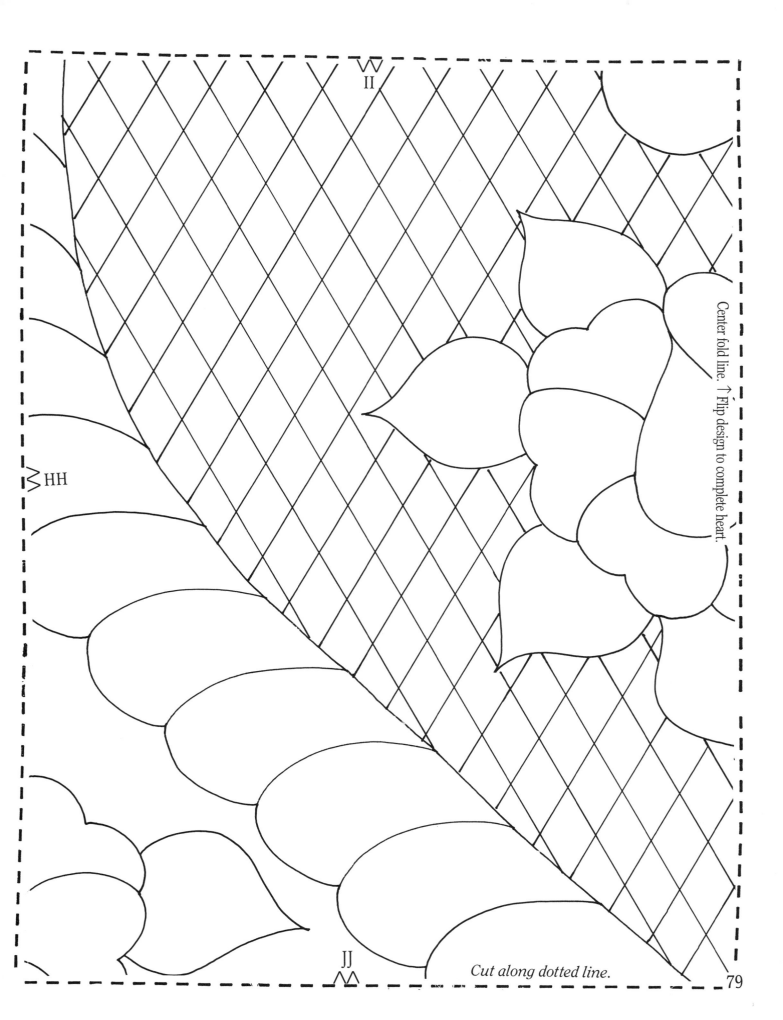

II

Center fold line. → Flip design to complete heart.

HH

JJ

Cut along dotted line.

79

One Dozen Roses Wall Quilt
Applique/Quilting Layout

Embroider berries with a satin stitch and berry stems with a stem stitch.
Use ¼″ bias tape or ½″ folded bias tape to create rose stem (or vine).

Cut along dotted line.

FF

II

Center fold line. → Flip design to complete heart.

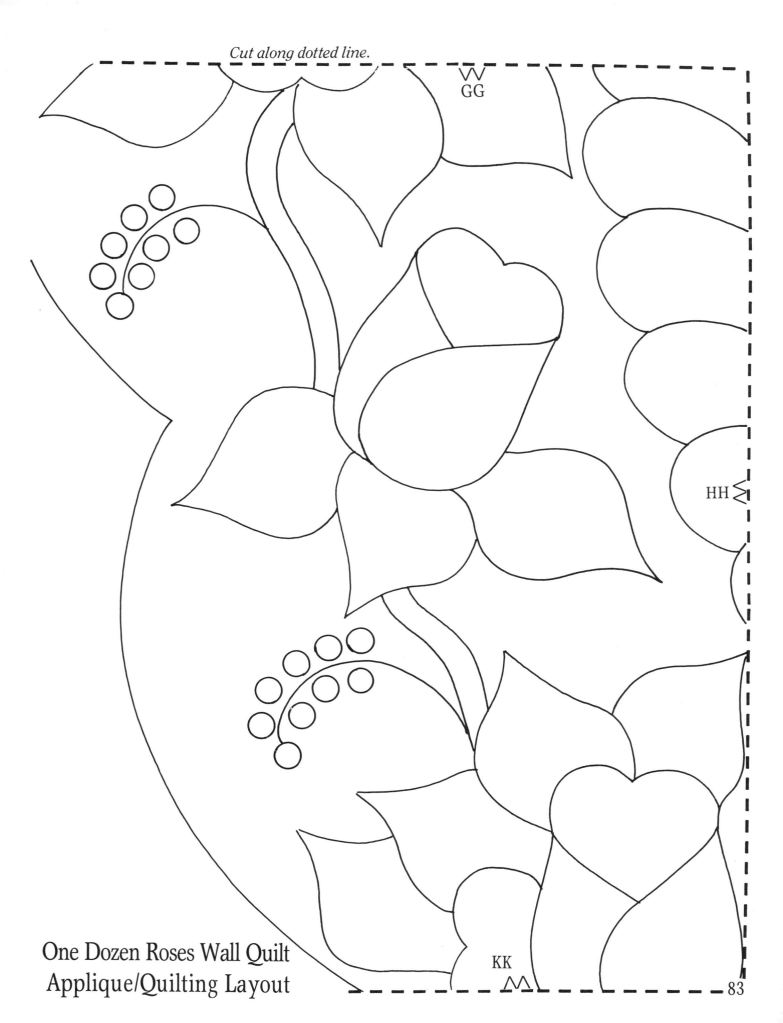

Cut along dotted line.

GG

HH

KK

One Dozen Roses Wall Quilt
Applique/Quilting Layout

83

JJ

LL

Center fold line. → Flip design to complete heart design.

Cut line to split design layout.

LL

KK

Cut along dotted line.

85

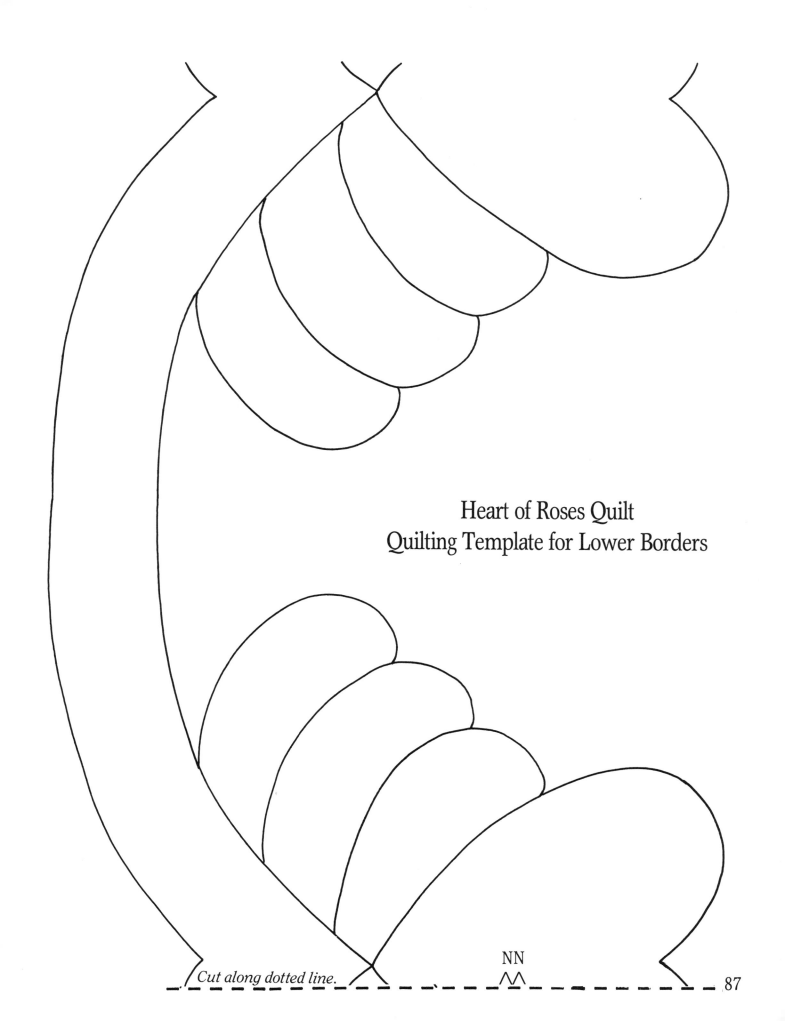

Heart of Roses Quilt
Quilting Template for Lower Borders

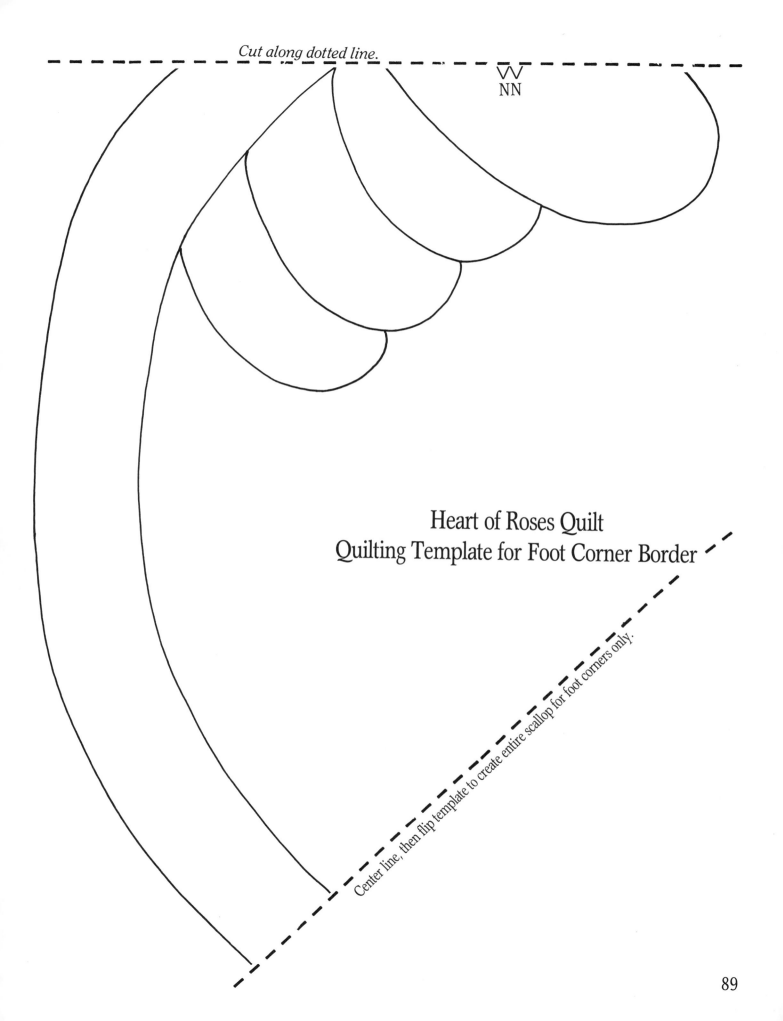

Cut along dotted line.

NN

Heart of Roses Quilt
Quilting Template for Foot Corner Border

Center line, then flip template to create entire scallop for foot corners only.

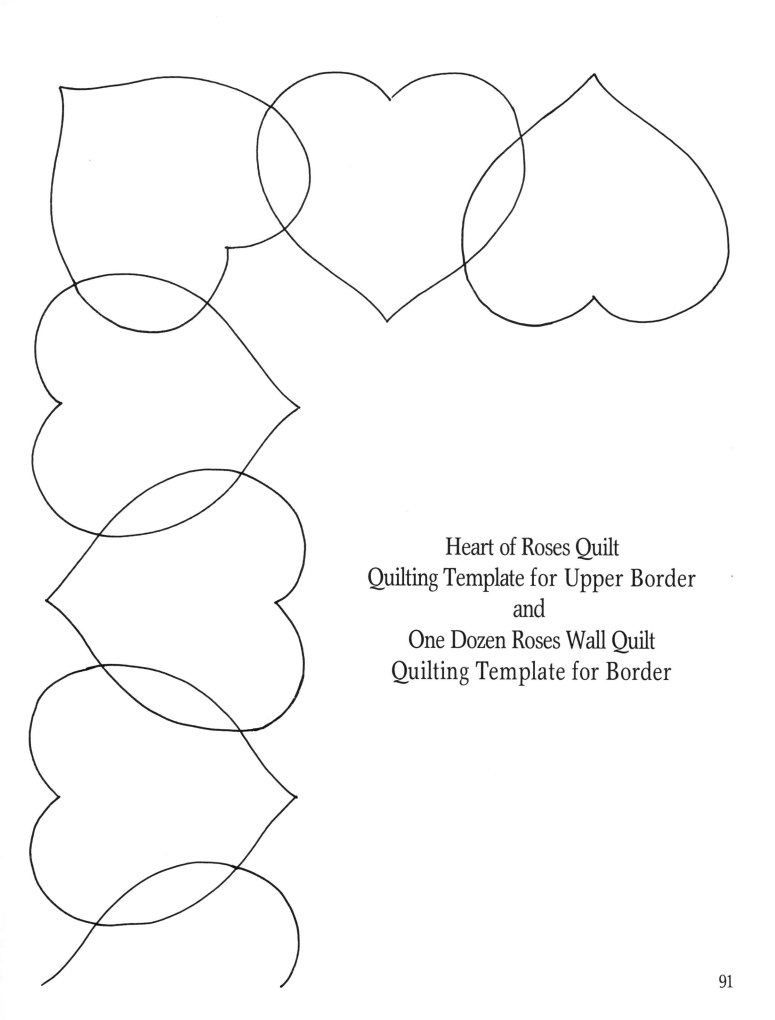

Heart of Roses Quilt
Quilting Template for Upper Border
and
One Dozen Roses Wall Quilt
Quilting Template for Border

This area can be used for the date and quiltmaker's name,
or it can be quilted with the ½" crosshatch pattern used in the center of the wall quilt (see page 79).

O R D E R F O R M

Background Fabric Pack for
The Heart of Roses Quilt

The Pack includes:

- 1 precut pillow throw with stenciled feather heart design
- 1 precut center panel with the following markings—large stenciled scalloped heart, stenciled center feather heart design, center rose with ½" and 1" crosshatching, and stenciled feather heart design in two lower corners.
- 1 precut bottom border
- 2 precut side borders
- 1 seamless quilt back of matching wide fabric (wider and longer than quilt top size)

All fabric is Ivory, 50% poly/50% cotton blend fabric, preshrunk, permanent press.
Please note: this is the background fabric only.

Packs are available in 4 sizes:

- King Mattress, 78" x 80"   —$89.00
- California King Mattress, 72" x 84"   —$89.00
- Queen Mattress, 60" x 80"   —$79.00
- Double Mattress, 54" x 75"   —$79.00

Also Available

- 3½-yards of 116"-wide fabric (Ivory, 50% poly/50% cotton blend), *uncut* and *unmarked*—$29.00

*(To have enough fabric for BOTH the top and back of a Heart of Roses quilt,
order TWO 3½-yard lengths.)*

(Please fill in the payment and shipping information on the other side.)

NUMBER OF PACKAGES	PACKAGE SIZE OR AMOUNT OF YARDAGE	PRICE	TOTAL
	PA residents add 6% sales tax		
	Shipping and Handling (Add 10%, $3.00 minimum)		
	TOTAL		

Method of Payment

☐ Check or Money Order
(payable to The Old Country Store in U.S. funds)

☐ Please charge my:
    ☐ MasterCard   ☐ Visa

#_____

exp. date _____

Signature _____

Name_____

Address _____

City _____

State_____

SHIP TO: *(if different)*

Name_____

Address _____

City _____

State_____

Zip _____

Mail order to **The Old Country Store**
P.O. Box 419, Intercourse, PA 17534-0419
Call toll-free 800/760-7171, In Canada call collect 717/768-7101
Fax number 717/768-3433

Prices subject to change.